HAPPILY EVER AFTER?

HAPPILY EVER AFTER?

Shared stories about love and marriage without the fairytale ending

XAVIA JONES, LYNDA WHEELER, NICOLE WHITE

Fifth Street Publishing INC

First Printing, 2022

Fifth Street Publishing Inc
fifthstreetpub.com

Table of Contents

I

Authors' Notes

This book contains real stories from individuals who have endured divorce or had a near divorce experience. The authors wanted the voice of each storyteller to be their own. Every story was told through the lens of each individual's experience. Their contribution consists of their work to share explicitly, the challenges and perspectives of their journey.

We, the authors, share the common ground of being divorcees. The birth of this book came from the desire to create a discussion, on a larger scale, of what we discovered while sharing our experiences. Through our varied backgrounds, we have found many levels of understanding. Some of the writers have requested to maintain anonymity, so while some names have been changed, the stories remain true.

This work takes sixteen questions that invites both the

writers and readers to dive into how their answers fit into the context of their journey.

I

Introduction

Happily ever after is an idiom that finds itself concluding romantic fairy tales suggesting that life will go on perfectly. Well, we know that life is all but a fairy tale and marriage is challenging. Sometimes you find that you're happy, after... after you find yourself on the other side of the deconstruction of what you thought your life would be and who you have become.

Statistically, half of all marriages in the US end in divorce. An unfortunate, yet common, situation that often leaves those involved feeling alone when they are faced with the reality of a broken marriage. Not all marital difficulties end in the finality of a divorce. Couples may reach the brink of ending their vows without following through with the legal dissolution of their marriage. Nonetheless, they face the same questions and challenges divorced people encounter.

Ultimately, whether you decide to repair or dissolve your marriage, it is necessary to grow and learn.

There isn't always an easy-to-find support group through these situations. There isn't a perfect method of how to process the difficulty during that season. What we can seek to find are others who have traveled the path and found happiness and peace on the other side of these challenging times.

What someone's journey looks like may differ from the next person's. However, what we found in being able to share stories is that there are quite a few similarities between individuals. In sharing these experiences, the sense of loneliness dissipates and camaraderie is formed. Where there are shared stories, there is human connection. As we share our vulnerability we begin to expose our humanity wherein lies the opportunity to grow and heal. In that place, we can seek to find an understanding of ourselves and others.

Esther Hicks, from the Abraham-Hick publications, has said that the basis of life is freedom; the purpose of life is joy; the result of life is growth. Our thoughts and attention garner our reality, so if we choose joy, it becomes our reality. Now, if this reality undergoes a change where we believe we are experiencing a form of trauma, supposedly we can shift our mindset to believe that joy will come eventually. This hope is the key to actually overcoming imperfect situations; situations such as the downfall of a marriage

We have formulated questions for this compilation based on what was asked of us by others who've witnessed our tribulations or from those who were, unfortunately, going through something similar. We started with the very essence of the reason most people come together in the first place; love.

What follows describes the selection of the questions. Brenee Brown said, " When we deny our stories, they define us. When we own our stories, we get to write the ending." Our stories are a collage of our experiences, and we decide how to share them with the world if we will share them at all. *Happily Ever After?* took sixteen questions that explore the before, during, and after marriage and asked our writers to dig deep.

I

⚜

The Questions

Where did your idea of love come from?

To formulate a consensus thought about love, we have to understand where our idea of love first stemmed from. We've all most likely witnessed love from someone or some outlet, so the question is from whom or from what? Was it Disney? Our parents? The neighbor? Old movies? Was it an amalgamation of all of them? I find that this question may be difficult for some to answer. It has caused some of our participants to wonder if they have ever witnessed love. Going back to the psychology of Galton's, nature vs. nurture, is love something that is fostered, or is it innate? Essentially, is it something we are born with or is it learned behavior?

One would think love is something typically felt or seen at home first. However, we all know that the family dynamic isn't black and white, and it is quite subjective. Some children, who are being raised in a single-family home, may not have had the opportunity to witness their single parent giving or receiving affection or love to another adult. So what example does that child have when they grow up and find themselves loving an individual? Sure they may have witnessed familial affection, but they could be missing out on recognizing a healthy, back and forth between two adults. Now, we all know that married couples are not a better example, they are just a different example.

This required our writers to examine how they fundamentally viewed the idea of love and how that enforced their beliefs about marriage.

Why did you get married?

This is a question that deserves a great deal of attention. Dissecting the "why", the motivation, the root of the, "Will you", and the, "Yes" will provide grounds for all the other questions in this work. Exploration of the emotions of that one moment the decision was made to join your life and all that came with it, to someone else's life, allows the emergence of love, joy, pain, pressure, and the societal norms that influenced your commitment.

Was it a simple decision, after years of cohabitation and kids? Was it something that seemed to make sense after being high school sweethearts? Was it expected? Was it for financial stability? Did you think it would make you whole? Or was it a complicated, agonizing, murky decision filled with red flags? The answer to "Why did you get married" sets the stage for *Happily Ever After?*

How did things fall apart?

This is a hard question for any audience, but particularly for the people involved in the divorce. Both people understand that there is a sense of loss, regardless of who's to blame... if there was anyone to blame. This gives our writers and readers the opportunity to reflect on not just why they got married, but also why they got a divorce or separated. Our writers have analyzed, to the best of their ability, the catalyst that drove them to the final decision to end or repair their marriage. In asking this question, we hope to give a voice to doubts, a voice to reasoning, and naturally a voice to personal truths.

Would you have handled the dismantlement differently?

Some of us fail to do the work needed to define who we are individually, without a significant other. Are we seeking out the things we lack by finding it in another person? Should people complete one another? Many of the questions here have been created and orchestrated because we now have hindsight, which turns out to be the best perspective.

In the midst of tribulation, we may find ourselves being rash, aggressive, and reactive. As we know, our initial reaction to a terrible situation is usually not the best response. We have the tendency to be in lack; lack of self-control, lack of common sense, or lack of self-respect. So asking the question, *how would you handle the dismantlement of your relationship differently?* it forces us to look at ourselves and not the other person. It goes along the idea that forgiveness is mainly for ourselves, again, not for the other person.

You would have to consider how or if your response played an integral part in the breakdown of your relationship. Essentially, in revisiting this question it is expected that you would have done some self-reflection or possibly had therapy. Now, we do understand that not all relationships end terribly, so it may be possible that you have experienced a peaceful and mutual separation. Even if this is the case, we'd like you to describe or think about how you concluded that you were no longer interested in living a shared life with your significant other.

When did you notice a change in yourself or your spouse prior to the divorce?

This is a question that forces you to be honest about the imperfections within your relationship. It could best be answered by reviewing who the culprit has been, and yes, it is possible for two people to be at fault. There are usually red flags that we brush off as coincidence or perhaps we were the ones who encouraged our spouse to step out of their comfort zone and try something new, which then caused a shift in their behavior. There could have been concerns prior to marriage, but we thought marriage would somehow change those issues. Was there verbal abuse that was frequently seen as sarcasm? Did someone pick up a new hobby? Switch shifts at work? Did someone suddenly put a lock on their phone?

Clichés are quite funny because most of the time they are spot on. Experiencing something new is exhilarating when it is something we want. In a marriage, if one person is finding enjoyment elsewhere and the other person feels left out, then trouble could be brewing. At this moment, a conversation needs to be had to address the imbalance. Oftentimes, those needed conversations are missed, leaving the opportunity for resentment to fester.

As we evolve as individuals our needs, wants, and perspectives change. More often than not, those differences aren't communicated. Every marriage goes through a shift. How you decide to handle the shift, determines the stability of your relationship.

Did you and your spouse exhaust all possibilities to repair your relationship?

Not many people get married with the goal of divorcing. I used to wonder what life would be like if divorce was illegal. There are couples who typically believe that death will be the only way out, due to that small clause in our wedding vows, which says, "til death do us part."

There is typically no sabbatical to be taken from marriage. People could separate and reconvene with one another after some "soul searching", however, many people fear that separation would allow the other person to find someone else. So instead of spending time apart to reflect, find ourselves, or go to therapy, we may cling to the other person, causing more harm than good. The result of clinginess is more frustration and less dignity. One thing we wanted people to consider with this question was, was divorce the best option for you? Here are a few questions for couples to consider when reviewing if all options had been exhausted before deciding to quit:

1. Did we pray about it together? (if you're spiritual-minded)
2. Did we go to therapy? (together or apart)
3. Did we read self-help books?
4. Did we attempt to consider what changes we needed to personally make?
5. Have we communicated our dissatisfaction with one another in a respectful manner?

What is the greatest lesson learned from divorce?

Nothing in life manages to occur without presenting us with a lesson, or at least we hope that we gain insight from our experiences. That insight could be about our own journey of how we identify with our place in the world or how we relate to other people. Sometimes, we don't discover what those insights or lessons are for what seems like an eternity. What we desire for our writers and readers to do with this question is to explore whether they've confronted their lessons, and if they did, what did their lesson teach them? How has that lesson impacted their journey?

What was your greatest area of growth?

What does it mean to experience growth? Does it mean that you learn from your situation? Do we hold true to the adage that if it doesn't kill you, it'll make you stronger? How do you determine if you've made movement in the right direction? While it may be a matter of perception, my belief is that everything is growing, and growth is an unbroken cycle in our lives. Divorce can produce unique growth within us, depending on your perspective on personal growth, and how you choose to approach life's difficulties.

Did you go through any phases or develop any habits?

Going through a divorce is a loss that carries similar emotions to experiencing a death. There is the loss of what you thought your future would be, not to mention many people face the dismantling of financial security and stability. Dr. Elisabeth Kubler-Ross's five stages of grieving depict the process of grieving which is very relatable after a divorce. Denial, anger, bargaining, depression, and acceptance are all important pieces to the journey of finding healing, and each stage holds value. The danger is in being stuck in a particular state or making major decisions based on the temporary emotions of grief. Because the person doesn't actually die, it becomes easy to mask the gravity of grief that results from this kind of loss.

In an effort to get to the acceptance stage, often people forgo honoring the previous stages. The entire process is necessary and useful. I found that the most important part of the healing process was to become more self-aware. Acknowledging the truths behind what you're feeling and doing, by getting to the "why" behind the choices being made. One of the biggest "whys" had to do with dating. For example, why was I entertaining someone I had no interest in being in a relationship with? More often than not the answer was loneliness.

The cliche "hoe phase", as it's sometimes called on the dating scene, has been normalized as a somewhat rite of passage for divorcees. It is the coming out, if you will, after getting through a divorce and getting your sea legs in the treacherous waters the single life has to offer. Some decide that they want to dive into it with no intention or consideration of the outcome. Some find themselves in this phase unknowingly after several short-term dating experiences. Some never partake, and then there are those who may indulge long term. There are many factors that go into how an individual may approach being newly single; for example, the age you were when you got married, what your moral positions are on dating and sex, and ultimately where you are in the grief process.

Not everyone's experiences are alike because not everyone has the same set of beliefs about how they want to approach future relationships. This question allows some self-reflection as to what habits or series of choices the writer found themselves making.

What coping mechanisms worked if you've experienced depression?

In sticking with the five stages of grief, you can find yourself in the depression part of the cycle of grief, then bounce back to denial, circle back to anger, and revisit bargaining, at any given time. Coping with emotions can take a level of self-awareness that may not come easy. Not everyone is readily able to truly understand their emotions, let alone be equipped to process healthy ways to cope. Creating a new normal that is a healthy representation of who you want to be, requires you to be very intentional. You have to do the work. What does that look like? It could mean going to therapy, involving yourself in activities that bring you peace, or acknowledging the areas where growth is needed.

Journaling, exercising, investing in self-care, and creating regiments help foster healthy habits that don't involve other people but help individuals tremendously. Coping skills are as important as learning to read or write. This is something that isn't always taught at home nor school. A lot of times the need for these skills aren't realized until much later in adulthood. Coping skills are necessary to understand so they can be taught to children who may be going through the process of divorce with their parents.

The idea is to find ways to avoid unhealthy habits. Those unhealthy habits may provide instant gratification, but in the long run it could cause more problems. Overspending, overeating, or using alcohol, for example, only mask the negative emotions that are left for you to deal with in the end. Dealing with complex emotions seems like a large task, but it is as simple as consistently investing the time to take care of your emotional needs.

The writers had the opportunity to share what allowed them to move toward a more peaceful state of mind during their process. They were able to identify how they coped, and in that way have gifted tools to help others.

Where are you in your philosophy on marriage?

What does it mean to be a husband or a wife? What your expectations are going into a marriage, can change significantly when you evolve as an individual. As you read the stories, the perspectives on the philosophy of marriage included much more insight into themselves. Also, the writers were able to reflect on what they were taught about marriage. Depending on how much you hold true to what you were taught, your experiences can shift how someone will approach the idea of marriage again. This may greatly evolve or even diminish.

Redefining the idea of marriage can be an instrumental part of the healing process. An individual will hopefully be able to identify the areas in their thought process that were helpful or harmful, and decide where to place these newfound ideas about themselves and marriage. For example, I was taught that women should be completely submissive and that men preferred women to be that way. Instead of throwing away the entire idea of marriage because being completely submissive did not serve me, I examined that notion and decided if I wanted to include it in my current marriage philosophy.

The construct of marriage doesn't always fit into traditional norms. A divorce could be the reason someone chooses the path of being single going forward. For others, they may choose to define a relationship as a partnership and remove the standard conventions of marriage. It takes time to reflect and fully grasp all the pieces that formulate a personal philosophy. The most important part is to be sure of what you decide and be authentic in your pursuit of living by the standards you set.

What is the worst advice you received from others while going through your separation or divorce?

Someone is always eager to give unsolicited, unhelpful advice. It could come with good intentions; it may be that it just isn't applicable or healthy for your healing process. Divorce can be a painful experience that involves making major life decisions through a highly emotional time. Sometimes we rely on others to guide us through uncharted territory, which can be helpful or can hinder the healing process.

Advice from others can cause someone to draw back and reflect on how to make the best choices throughout the process, or it can just cause them to draw back and isolate themselves. It is important to seek out advice from those who truly have your best interest at heart and from those who have a noteworthy sense of self-awareness. At the end of the day, you have to discern what is applicable to you and what does not benefit your journey.

What was the best advice given to you?

People find clarity and connection through identifying with others. It goes without saying that during our most beautiful or tragic circumstances, our friends, family, and even people we are barely acquainted with, will offer advice; whether it is solicited or not. The true life-changing moments come when someone is able to offer a perspective which opens our own vantage point into circumstances. We are communal by nature and seek to relate to each other, and empathizing seems to be a way to do that.

Would you get married again?

This question is not as simple as it seems. Another way to interpret this question would be, was your situation traumatic enough to deter you from seeking love again? Then you must ask, do you believe in love anymore? Did you believe in it before? For others, marriage is the main objective, and finding the right person is a matter of opportunity. Ultimately, your philosophy is what drives you to embark on the journey once again.

Do you think you and your ex-spouse could be friends down the road?

Inherently you would think the majority of people would say, "HELL NO!" It was important to be inclusive of all types of endings. Not every divorce consists of bitter exchanges and never-ending custody battles. For the sake of children, couples are motivated to dissolve their marriage amicably. Others truly develop a deep consideration for one another's growth and happiness. In that, they are able to leave the union with a friendship and mutual respect.

That may seem like a lofty goal for couples who weren't ready for the ending of their marriage or felt a sense of betrayal that would cause the demise of the relationship. Sometimes it just behooves the two individuals to move forward, for them to completely move on and end any possible communication so that they are able to heal and start their journey into a new life.

For couples who decide to give their marriage a new start after separation, the idea of friendship takes on a different meaning. Reaching the brink of divorce essentially means that things needed to change in order to embark on the idea of starting over with each other. Massive repair suggests that there has to be realignment in how each person views the other in order to start over. That can fundamentally happen through a cultivated friendship.

Share one piece of advice with someone going through a divorce.

The premise behind the book is to create a sense of connection. Through that connection, the goal is to provide ease of comradery while facing a challenging situation. Whether you are newly divorced or seeking insight on how to conquer difficult emotions, we want every reader to have turned the last page feeling hopeful and united in the pursuit of healing and self-awareness. It isn't always easy to find purpose behind painful situations. However, if we hold on to the idea that our difficulties may help someone down the road, it can create a sense of value. We wanted each writer to be able to give back. Using their experience, it was important to give the opportunity to help both reader and writer express a specific point of reference that was most helpful.

THE STORIES

"Loving ourselves through the process of owning our stories is the bravest thing we will ever do."

-Brene Brown

II

Lakia's Story

"Why did I get married," it is the famous question everyone asks. Tyler Perry even had to make a play and a movie, I'm sorry, two movies about this. What can I say, I'm a hopeless romantic who wants the *American Dream*: husband, kids, and the nice house with a white picket fence. I know it's corny, but it's true. I was sold on the *American Dream*, and so was he. We meshed well and it was great. He wanted to be the provider, and have his wife as a partner that allowed him to lead. I really loved that man. Well, I still love him. I wish no ill will on him. I'm just not IN love with him anymore.

I have loved him since the first time I met him. I was just drawn to him. Seriously, I couldn't even explain it. He was so sexy-that smile. I met him when I was seventeen. He was eighteen. He was just street enough, if you know what I mean. We were so similar. We both loved music and theater. We were both from working families and divorced parents. We had so much in common. We became friends instantly, but nothing more because he was already dating someone, and I guess I was too... his best friend. No judgment, it was high school, okay! We never crossed any lines until years later, but I had a crush on him since the day I met him. We became best friends. Hanging out from time to time. We talked all the time. I wish I could say college took us separate ways, but nope. He ended up in the same state as me. We even ended up back in Chicago at the same time. Sounds like fate right. Well, all that glitters ain't gold. We dated, then moved in with each other. He proposed to me on my 25th birthday.

I was so shocked. We talked about marriage, but it was always distant talk. Nonetheless, I was happy that I was going to be Mrs. York. Unfortunately, after the engagement, things started to go downhill. I lost my job and his hours were unstable at work. We were in a new apartment on our own, with a baby, his; we had custody of his son. He started to feel that stress and started to withdraw from me. Conversations were nonexistent. I got a job- a better job. However, what I thought was just the stress of money problems happened to be deeper and I could not figure out what it was. I knew things were really bad when we had a huge snowstorm, and we were separated for three days. While I was worried sick and missed my best friend he was not fazed by the distance. When he was finally able to return home, the excitement was not there.

He started sleeping on the couch. He used the excuse that he had just fallen asleep on the couch because he was so tired. It was excused the first and second time, but when that became a nightly occurrence, I realized that I could not repair or even move forward when I was not aware things were broken. I was left feeling abandoned and shut out. We had not had sex in months. My final attempt was for us to reset and start a road to repair. I planned a whole night for us to get the sexy back in our relationship.

We weren't even married yet. So after that rejection and that abandonment of being shut out, how did ya'll end up married you may ask. Man, was I in love with that man. After almost a year we were finally physically in each other's presence, and it was clear that the spark was not gone no matter how hard we tried to ignore it.

One day we found ourselves at a mutual community picnic. He wanted to make it known we were there together even though we came separately. He walked across that picnic and kissed me right in the mouth. I mean that kiss you see in all the Disney movies that change the whole movie, the happy ending. We left the picnic together, went to dinner, and talked for hours like no time had passed at all. We went back to his house and made love all night. Back together we were. We talked about why we split; me saying I was lost and confused, and him saying it was not me, it was him. He was in his head and didn't know how to express a lot of his feelings and emotions. He didn't know how to control them, so he just shut me out. He promised I was all he ever wanted. That's why we were there. I loved him so much and was scared to lose him again. At that moment I gave him an ultimatum; if you want me, you will make me your wife. I'm not going to date you for another 5 years, I told him. His response was much like Dr. McDoogle from *Sex In the City*, "Alrighty." Sad, but true.

I don't know if things were ever put back together before we even got married. We had already been split for almost a year. We would show up at get-togethers separately and leave together. People gossiped but were happy to see us back together and planning a wedding. Everyone felt we were meant for each other. I just wanted to be married to him so bad. We settled on getting married at the courthouse instead of the downtown Hilton. I just wanted, and needed to be Mrs. York.

As time went on, it got to the point where love doesn't pay the bills. Money got too tight...too tight. He was short on hours, and I had to work overtime to pick up the slack. My family became a burden to him. He spoke at me, not to me and I just shut down. I was so fearful to say anything that might make him leave me. He hated that I didn't talk enough, and he felt like I wasn't putting him first because I did so much for my family.

I found out he was cheating and disrespectfully communicating with her sexually while I was at home. That shit hurts. Even still after that, I tried. I tried and he still rejected me. I mean what other options do we have when the other party is not willing to participate in trying to make it work?

If I could change things, I wouldn't have allowed it to go as long as it did. I wish I would have said something earlier. I would have started making plans for myself earlier, and not have begged that man for a damn thing. No one should have to beg for love, especially, when my actions were not the main cause of our breakup. He cheated and I begged him to come back. I was one desperate chick. No way I would do that again.

Coping after the separation was hard. Every moment was

a struggle- being without him, not able to speak with him. We usually would talk all day. He was my best friend. I had some low days, but I'm happy that my support system would not allow me to be alone. I made sure I was occupied. I went out with friends, staying out all night like back when I was in college. My Papa was a huge savior though. I moved back in with my dad after we separated. My Papa had recently moved in too. We became so close in that short time. He's my step-mother's father, so I didn't grow up with him, but I swear you couldn't tell. He treated me just like I was birthed by his own daughter. He would take me to all his old spots on the block. We drank, played pool, and danced all night long at least 3 times a week. On other days we would sit, watch NCSI, and finish a bottle of wine while we talked. I miss those long nights, talking with him.

Sleeping alone was the worst though. Going back into that room every night to an empty bed was the worst. But, sleeping around just wasn't my thing. I wasn't the serial dating type, I'm a relationship person. I like the one person you get to learn inside and out monogamy. I slept out a lot of nights just so I wouldn't have to sleep in my bed alone, our marital bed. I slept on a lot of couches or drank too much so that I couldn't even figure out I was in bed alone.

You usually hear about the guys, and their break-up baby, but it was the female this time, and I'm okay with that, because that's what I needed. I really needed that to let go. Crazy, I know, I had the breakup baby.

I prayed for a release from my ex-husband. I made that man my everything. It was hard coping without being able to talk to him every day. The church was a lot of help. We had started going back to church regularly before our separation. I attended more church events and classes. It was easy to pour myself into the church and I was happy to go alone. It was my time to be able to lay all my burdens down because every day was a struggle. I'm soooo happy I didn't give up on church.

Music was such a big help. Isaac Caree's album, *Reset*, had just come out and I was addicted. What a perfect title, *Reset*. At that time my life seriously needed a reset. I prayed for a reset. I needed a clean break, a new world where my failed marriage wouldn't even be on my mind. Man, they say watch what you pray for. It may not come in the way you want or how you thought it would be, but he is always right on time.

Right on time was the coldest day of the year. I totaled my car, T-boned by a semi. The State trooper wouldn't even walk up to my car because he thought I was dead. Nobody, but God. The paramedic let me have my phone in the ambulance. I had Issac Carree playing on the speaker. *Give me one good reason why you should still be alive. That accident you passed last night was meant to take your life.* I was bawling like a baby. Then, I got to the hospital. I had a routine pregnancy test before I went into x-rays in order for them to remove my neck collar and unstrap me from the board. Still, in tears, I was so confused and distraught. God allowed me to walk out of the hospital that day with only a black eye, a few bruises, stitches, and a perfect fetus. It still blows my mind when I think about it.

That was my reset. That was my out. I had to focus on this baby that was growing inside of me, so had no time for him. I had put this man and what we had so far out of my mind that I told him I was pregnant on our second-year anniversary.

Seems cold-hearted, I know, but I swear it was not malicious. I seriously wasn't even aware of the day or date. I had been debating about telling him before our divorce hearing. I leaned toward the fact that it was none of his business. At the date of our divorce hearing, I was six months pregnant. I decided to tell him then. He didn't take it well. I think it was the nail in the coffin. He knew at that time this relationship was dead, dead. No coming back. It was extra hard for him because he told me later that one of the biggest things he wanted from me was another baby. I wanted that too-our child, half me, half him, that bond. When it came down to it, I told him no. I denied my husband the one big thing we both wanted. I couldn't. I just couldn't bring myself to do it when we were falling apart.

We tried to be friends. Funny thing is, we actually tried to rekindle recently. We felt that the time apart allowed us to grow into the people we needed to be while we were together. They say time apart can bring folks closer together. We tried. For over a year we tried. We even took our first vacation together out of the country. Promising each other to do bigger and better things. That caught fire quickly and died. The distance made it difficult. He is in Arkansas and I'm in Illinois. After that trip to Cancun, we fought more than we did when we were married. We had a loud screaming match that ended with me leaving Cancun with bruises. I realized I was back in the same place I was when we were together. Actually, worse off because he had never put his hands on me. I was completely turned off and unfortunately, there was no coming back from that. We cannot be friends. That seriously was the end of anything we could have ever had. It made me recall that lesson that I thought I learned when we divorced. "Don't let a man tell you he doesn't want you more than once." Favorite line from Judge Lynn Toler. I have been rejected by that man time in and time out.

I still believe in marriage. However, I know it's going to take me some time to get to that place where I can trust again. I still want that partnership and companionship, that love. I want to be loved and wanted by my spouse.

Why is it when people hear of a breakup, they always want to lend their feelings about your situation and tell you what they would have done? They say, oh no, that couldn't have been them this could have happened to. Like, what's the deal? Shut up! Oh, and please stop telling folks to go be hoes, to just go out and smash anything and anyone they want. Like, what? What are you thinking telling a person that is broken from this breakup to go entangle all those feelings into sex with random people? Not a good suggestion at all.

Self-love was the best advice I received. Focus on you and heal yourself. Stop thinking about what others think. Stop listening to them telling you should get back out there. Do you, and heal.

I would absolutely get married again, I am still a hopeless romantic. I crave that love, that parentship, that companion-ship. I'm so happy my experience has not changed my outlook on marriage, but it has allowed me to look at people and situations differently. I found my pattern and I'm happy I was able to recognize it. So many people are oblivious to their pattern. I've always been the pursuer. I have never been pur-sued. I look forward to approaching it differently by allowing it to approach me. I have to create a whole me and when I am at that place, he will find me. God's timing, is right.

My greatest area of growth has been self-love. If I could leave a piece of advice for those who are going through a divorce, just take it one day at a time. This is just a moment in your life, a phase of events. Don't allow it to end your life and make you cynical. There is a blessing in your lesson. It hurts me deeply hearing people say they will never marry again. Like, don't give up on love. Everyone is not your ex. Every man is not the same. If you keep running into the same man, it's you baby. You keep attracting the same person. You haven't made the change you needed to make yet. Love is a beautiful thing. Everyone deserves love. I believe that you attract what you give out. Repair yourself, you have to be whole before you can pour into anyone else. Always be working on self. Also, understand people will not love the way you love.

~ Lakia York

Lakia's story highlights the hopefulness and persistence love can drive even against your better judgment. She relentlessly pursued her idea of what she felt was the American dream. While she has not been deterred from her pursuit of happily ever after, she is now more equipped to approach the idea of love as a wiser woman.

"Sharing our truths can provide the opportunity for great healing."

-Kristen Noel

III

Breanna's Story

I believe that marriage is something profound that a lot of people don't take seriously. I feel it's dismissed, and a lot of people want to be married just to say, "I'm married." I don't believe people understand the importance and value that marriage holds. My outlook on marriage is a whole one. I believe it is wanting to see that person smile every day and doing everything in your power to make it so. To think of loving a person more than you love yourself. To cherish them, understanding and desiring to take care of them financially, mentally, and emotionally. To talk when there is a problem. To not wake up the next day mad or go to sleep mad at each other. If there is a problem, it can be fixed because if it's no problem, then there's no problem. I feel couples should treat each other equally, and care enough about what each other is dealing with or going through. A marriage can be different and difficult but if you love each other so much, that love can outweigh the bad.

My idea of love came from when I was younger watching movies like, *The Titanic* or *Pretty Woman*. It was the way the men looked at the women in those movies that made you know it was real; it was something I wanted to experience and have for the rest of my life.

I got married because he was the love of my life, and I wanted to spend the rest of my life with him. I had been with him since I was fifteen and thought, who could make me happier than him? He used to be everything to me, did everything for me, and when you saw him you saw me when you saw me you saw him. We were irresistible to each other. Bonnie and Clyde, but not killers, ha! Everything fell apart when he began to get physically abusive. It happened for years on and off, but I always believed he was sorry. I always believed he would change. I always forgave his lies even when I knew deep down, I deserved better. The day I left was when our son got in one of our fights and he told his father, "If you hit my mom again, I'm gonna fight you." He couldn't have been but 9 years old, but he had had enough, and I had to get out. That wasn't anything I wanted my kids to see, and I had to love my kids more than that relationship. I left and I've never been back. My mental state was great when I got in the relationship, but after years I was just in the relationship for my kids because I always wanted to raise my children in a two-parent home.

My marriage changed when my partner became the bread-winner in our home. When I became pregnant with our first child, we decided I would stay home to be a mother and a wife. I did everything but make the money. I've always had savings for a rainy day, but knowing this would only be a transition, I chose to leave my savings alone.

After I gave birth to our second child, I went to school for my CNA license. I got the kids up and ready for school, did homework with them, and cared for them. I cooked, cleaned, and did laundry. I made sure everything was perfect by the time he came home. I did this when I was working and when I wasn't. Can you imagine what one woman can do? I started to feel that he thought that since he paid the bills he could come and go as he pleased, and he did not have to spend the quality time he once did. He never asked me how I was feeling or if I needed anything, and the time he spent with the kids was not there either. After I told him about himself, we began to argue more than talk or make love or kiss or touch each other. He started to turn me off, and I don't think he cared. He thought since we had been together since I was fifteen and I was pregnant with our third child, that I was not going anywhere.

I remember noticing a change in me when I didn't want to be around people, I lost weight, my energy was blah, and I slept a lot. He was weighing on me and I didn't like it. I exhausted all possibilities before walking away after every chance I gave him by staying and hoping he would see how much we loved and needed him, but he let the drugs, the women, and the money get to him.

The greatest takeaway from my divorce is the hope of leaving on good terms, hoping it will not be messy or end up in court. Which it didn't. The greatest area of growth is loving yourself more and putting yourself and your children first. I've grown to live on my own and let it just be me and my children.

The worst advice I was given, was to call the police and press charges. The best advice I was given, was to walk away if he was unable to stop what he was doing to us. The only bad thing about leaving my relationship was that for months my kids wanted their daddy and they wanted him to come home, and I would always say, no. Of course, when they would get with their daddy, he would always tell them, "Your mom doesn't want me there." So, he made me seem like a bad person for years. At one point, I thought my kids hated me for not allowing their dad home, when in reality, they forgot the fights and did not understand that I was saving them and myself. The best advice I can give a person is, no matter how much you love or like a person, or don't want to be alone, NEVER IGNORE THE SIGNS, leave!

~ Breanna Douglas

Breanna's story reminds us that there are always signs that prompt us when change is needed. Her happily ever after was specifically designed around the best interest of her children. She worried that her children wouldn't understand her choices but ultimately realized how resilient they are.

"Forgiveness is an act of self-love"

-Don Miguel Ruiz

IV

Demond's Story

My Mother passed from kidney failure at the age of forty-three, I was fourteen years of age at her passing. I was taken care of by my family who showed me that love overshadows the bad that every family deals with. My family is very close and I was blessed to be born into it. My grandparents set the tone long ago. I have aunts who've divorced but I still consider their exes my "uncles" and they, still to this day, call me "nephew."

Why I got married is an intricate question. I was definitely in love and could see myself spending the rest of my life with her. However, having to make that decision at that time was scary. I was always confident in knowing I'm a good man, but a good husband was another thing. I was very fortunate and blessed to have all children by the same woman who eventually became my wife. So, I can confidently say I got married for love and to start my family.

Even though we had two children before "tying the knot," I felt that marriage was actually the beginning, even though most feel it's the final step. Becoming a father was a level of growth that required selflessness, but the idea of serving a wife and children, I felt, would be an even greater task of learning selflessness.

The "falling apart" phase is one that isn't noticed sometimes until after it happens. Being transparent, infidelity played a role in the falling apart, in addition to wanting different things at that time in our lives. I believe also a ton of attention was put on my children. Though we did things as a family, I feel like a wife desires separate and specific attention to wants and needs. Another reason was separate dreams. My spouse wanted to relocate and start fresh in a different atmosphere. This did sound doable, and you'd think it would be an easy choice. Not in my situation. I had a career at the time where I felt it wouldn't be smart to just leave on a wing and a prayer. I currently await retirement soon from the same position, so I did not just want to abandon that position for a risk my spouse wanted to take. I felt like as the "man" of the house, I was making the appropriate decision for the "unit". Not just saying, no, because I just didn't want to relocate. It felt like the right adult decision.

I believe we exhausted all possibilities. We agreed that we were both young, and still had a lot of life left to live. It's difficult to live in uncertainty and walk around on eggshells. At the peak of our union, we lived with no doubt that this was where we wanted to be and how we wanted to be. We didn't want a union without that element. I understand now why separation can be lengthy because you're trying to see if reconciliation is possible before the divorce.

Divorce doesn't have to be nasty. No one wins in divorce, so winning a divorce shouldn't be the goal. I learned not to make decisions during emotional episodes, to take time to heal, and not to take everything so personal. People ultimately want happiness and have to realize no one can give that to you and on the flip side, no one should be able to take it away. Having your children see emotional intelligence, understanding, forgiveness, and strength displayed during the process will help all parties involved.

After separation, I did notice my purpose had weakened. When you lack purpose you engage more in pleasure. I did find myself at that roadblock. Thankfully, it was noticed and a proper readjustment was made.

Coping tactics are huge! I'm grateful that my coping tactics were positive ones. Being accountable and not just pointing the finger was a major plus in coping. Being a musician, music has always been therapeutic for me. Working out my body for physical health and wellness in addition to my mind for emotional wellness, wisdom, and growth. Being an amazing father to my wonderful children also helped in coping. There were moments I felt that I failed as a husband, but as a father, I'd never fail!

I've grown a great deal in many areas since the divorce. One of the greatest areas is empathy. Differentiating when something is done to me and when something happens to me. Sympathy is understanding something from my own perspective. Empathy is putting myself in the other person's shoes and understanding why a particular decision was made. Not taking things so personal allows me to avoid defense mode which usually ends in an argument or disagreement.

I believe marriage is a beautiful thing. It takes a level of commitment and selflessness that one must have or adapt, to benefit all parties involved. I came up in an era where the phrase, " happy wife happy life" was the goal almost. I disagree with that term now. I believe it's one-sided and gives false expectations of how marriage should be. A husband's happiness is equally important. Marriage isn't the goal for some, but for many it is. I don't want anyone to feel that they've failed because they're not married at a certain point in life. Also, not to feel that they've failed if the divorce was a choice. I'm aware of a lot of marriages that are "done" while still in the midst of living a shared life. Couples staying together for financial reasons, for the kids, worried about how they're viewed by others if they divorce, etc. I believe staying in something you no longer want to be in, for someone else, probably has the opposite effect of what's expected. I do understand different situations call for specific decisions, but ultimately I believe happiness is essential to life however that may look for you.

I can't say that I got any bad advice or maybe I tuned it out, depending on the source. I'm a pretty private person so going through my separation I only trusted individuals who knew, from my mouth, the specific circumstances. These are individuals I go to when things are good just as they are bad. No one knows your specific situation like you and your spouse, so I'm not one to seek advice from a number of people, because it's mostly coming from a place of what they'd do in a situation as such. So, I try my best to take the liberty of owning a situation, like marriage, and make my own decisions because again, it is my marriage.

The best insight came from the two people I trust with my life, my aunt and uncle. They took over guardianship of me when my mother passed. So they're like my parents. They let me know that divorce doesn't mean failure. They gave me the support I needed while allowing my spouse and I to make our decision regarding our future. They let my spouse know they'll love her as they always have. Our differences have nothing to do with how they feel about her. They helped soften the blow for our children as well. They encouraged me to continue to be a great father and great man! Don't lose dignity in this situation! As I look back, that advice was golden!

I never like to say, never, but the desire to be married again is not there. I now know that marriage doesn't dictate my degree of love for someone who's special to me. I can say that my ex and I are friends today. It takes maturity, accountability, empathy, understanding, strength, and other variables that are good for your personal growth simultaneously to strengthen your "new" relationship with an ex, especially if children are involved. Getting along and co-parenting effectively is so important. We communicate well and our strong passion for the greatness of our children together is a common goal, not retaliation or making anyone hurt. Acknowledging the past, but not living in it, is another key point. This is a woman I once felt I couldn't live without, the mother of my children, so respect is a must. When it's given and demanded it sets the tone for the partnership now.

In closing, I want to reiterate how important forgiveness, accountability, and empathy are when going through a divorce. Winning should not be the goal, instead, understanding, cohesiveness, and prosperity, in an unfortunate situation, should be the goal. Divorce shouldn't define you any more than marriage should. Divorce isn't the end of your story. It's a chapter in your book of life. I'm still writing...I love the triumphs from adversity. This story should be told and shared. We avoided the stereotypical, "bitter divorce" label and the "bitter ex" stigmas. We want the best for one another even if we're not the specific ones that can provide it to one another. It's still deserving! That's love!

~Demond Nicks

Demond's story depicts the idea that although differences may be irreconcilable, taking the path of building separate lives can be harmonious. As he details, the work of accountability, transparency, and forgiveness was his happily ever after. The work to get to that place was purposeful and allowed for self-reflection which led to personal growth. His story shows that when you seek to understand others you find peace within yourself.

"The journey to self-love and self-acceptance must begin with self-examination."

-Iyanla Vanzant

V

Xavia's Story

For most of my childhood, I was raised by a single mother. I was my mother's first child and my father's only child. They were never married. I fantasized about having a perfect family with my husband, but after heartache I realized that my children needed to see me happy and emotionally healthy.

I came from a big family on my mother's side. Some of my aunts were married or in a long-term relationship, and I had a few uncles who were married and divorced. For the most part, not many stayed together long enough to provide an example of what a solid marriage looked like. Most marriages I did witness were filled with unhealthy interactions, which ultimately skewed my perception of relationships.

My mom married my step-father when I was nine. Because my mom was a single mother, I essentially went on all their dates with them and had a front-row seat as they formed their relationship. This was the first time I saw a couple exhibit mutual respect and love for one another.

At a young age, I knew that I wanted a family structure that emulated the complete opposite of what I grew up seeing. It was important to me to have one husband with whom I'd raise my children with. So when I found myself pregnant in my junior year of high school, I automatically thought about marrying my then-boyfriend. I was a child with a very grown-up responsibility of being a mother.

My ex and I both grew up in very religious homes, so we carried the guilt of trying to do what was right in the sight of God and for our parents. We tried to stay together, but that only ended up being a very tumultuous relationship. The fights I grew up seeing between my grandparents, aunts' and uncles' relationships were acted out in mine until life unexpectedly halted for us. My firstborn child tragically died at the age of two. Then, fifteen days later we had a second son. Before we lost our firstborn child our relationship had ended. Although I was pregnant with our second child, I was looking for my own place and he was in a relationship with someone else. However, stricken by grief we were forced to cling together. We thought our tragedy was a calling to be better for our second son. My now oldest child was two months old when we decided to get married. We felt marriage atoned for our sins and we became very focused on our faith and trying to be the perfect Christian family.

Trauma and tragedy bonded us together. We were two deeply broken and wounded individuals who came together with a vast misunderstanding of what it was to have a healthy marriage. We attempted to read all the books, go to counseling, and us going to church was a constant. Nonetheless, the pain of being wounded always resurfaced. Our relationship was toxic before my son died, and my ex used the tragedy to validate his resentment.

At some point, I realized that things would never change. No matter how much I prayed, no matter how much I tried to be perfect or accommodating, the marriage would not be fixed. Once things became unbearable I decided I could no longer carry the heaviness of my destructive marriage. I snapped... I did not go crazy or hurt anyone. I just went to work and never went back to the home we shared. I lived my life trying to be what everyone thought I should be, so leaving the way I did was the breakdown of the facade I maintained for so many years. It was freeing. I never knew how heavy the weight I carried was until I no longer had to bear the load. I learned how to be my authentic self and that was the greatest lesson. Setting boundaries was unfamiliar to me and took a lot of work to consistently make myself aware of my boundaries, and to be able to communicate what my boundaries were to other people.

Looking back, I don't know if I had the capacity to handle things differently. I knew my marriage was over three years before it ended. Truthfully, the marriage was fundamentally doomed before it even started. I suppressed my feelings of anger and hurt, thinking I could manage until my children were older. That was not sustainable. After attending therapy one day, I opened up about all the painful events that took place in my marriage, and like a dam with a crack in it, the impounded emotions burst and I was never the same.

I continued therapy which gave me the tools I needed to

help navigate through my divorce. I "found myself" by latching on to family and friends. I had to discover who I was. Since I had been a mother from the age of seventeen years old, I had to become familiar with Xavia- the woman. Adventure, reading, and traveling helped me discover some amazing things about myself. There is life after divorce. I heard that over and over, and it helped me along the way.

With my roots strongly planted in my faith, I was thrown scripture that had me second-guessing my decision to leave. "God hates divorce," was the one that was told to me. It was a pastor who validated my choice and enlightened me that, "God also hates violence," and he equipped me with scripture, and strengthened my ability to better my perspective about my situation.

Being that I had never experienced dating as an adult, I was completely clueless as to how to navigate the dating scene. Unclear of what I wanted and terrified of commitment, I found myself giving in to my loneliness and boredom. That only led to disappointment and heartache. I love LOVE and believe in marriage for those who choose to embark on that journey. I now have a vastly different understanding of what marriage is and I have shifted my expectations. My hope is to find my person; a love with a commitment that is mutually respectful and passionate- it doesn't have to fit into the construct of marriage. I am patient enough to make sure that it's right and I am prepared to receive what I desire.

My marriage had some good moments within the chaos, but the emotional scars were deep and the disrespect was unbearable. Nothing is unforgivable in my eyes. I can only hope that my children are equipped with the tools to work through the baggage that comes along with divorced parents, but we will not be friends. We had an unhealthy marriage and a grievous divorce, however, I am truly grateful for my four beautiful children.

My best advice would be to start new traditions and rituals for yourself and your children. I have a Friday night tradition with my kids to cook together and then watch a movie. I also started a tradition with my friend to go out every other weekend for a small girls' night. These things provide something to look forward to and help you find little joys that can be tremendously helpful.

~ Xavia Jones

Xavia's story is one that tells about the courage to choose you. The ability to let go of guilt and shame to pursue a healthier more peaceful life isn't selfish, but takes a level of audacity and fearlessness. Her un-fairytale ending is realizing that life is perfectly imperfect. She came to the understanding that two halves don't make a whole person, it makes a mess. She realized that in order to be whole she had to remove herself from the toxicity to truly appreciate her authentic self.

"Sometimes you have to do what you have to do
to survive in order to do what you were created to do."

-TD Jakes

VI

◉❦❦◉

Sophia's Story

I have been married for twenty-seven years to the man I had a crush on during my teenage years. I am a licensed professional counselor and I work in the mental health field. I am one of fourteen; seventh oldest. My siblings and I grew up with two parents in the home; whereas, our mother ruled with an iron fist and our father was very passive. Our father was a functional alcoholic and our mother beat us over the head with the Bible. Both parents are deceased.

I left my parent's home when I was eighteen years old. As it was with most of my siblings, we were eager to leave the nest when we were of age. After living with my oldest sister for a while, and then my brother and his family for a while, I decided I was ready to have my own. At twenty years old, I moved into my own apartment. I had my own car and my own money. I felt accomplished. I later dated a man, Antoine, who at the time was in college full time and very enthused about learning, so much so that it rubbed off on me. I began what ended up as a stop-and-start twenty-year journey in pursuit of my education. I finally graduated with my Masters in counseling in 2013. A lot happened during that time span. Antoine and I had a child. This was my oldest daughter. Antoine and I did not marry. We were in a relationship for eight years before I decided to end the relationship and move on. Shortly thereafter, I met Darryl. After about six months of dating, we moved to Colorado and married in the courthouse.

Darryl was my first husband. We both had children from our previous relationship. Darryl and I both were searching for happiness and new beginnings. We both were looking for love in a lasting relationship. At twenty-nine years old, I felt my biological clock ticking and I did not want to grow old alone. So, when Darryl asked me to move to Colorado and marry him; I did. I packed up, and my daughter and I rode the train to Colorado to meet Darryl. Darryl had gone before us to start working his new job. He was able to secure a home using my section-8 voucher. As a single parent, I took advantage of the support that was made available to low-income single parents. When my daughter and I arrived in Colorado; Darryl and I set up to begin living our lives in a beautiful state with new beginnings. I enrolled my daughter in preschool. I was able to find a job right away working as a receptionist for the Small Business Administration. Daryll had found a nice church in Littleton, Colorado which we attended on Sundays. The drive from Denver to Littleton was amazingly beautiful. Daryll, my daughter, and I went on lots of drives touring the beautiful mountains and admiring the wonders of the land. Things were great. I met Darryl's family who lived in Colorado. They all seemed to be doing very well for themselves. Daryll introduced me to his new friends. We were starting to build a circle of mutual friends. This lasted all of two to three months. Daryll had got a second job working as a bouncer in a club.

This did not work well for our marriage, especially since Daryll struggled with drinking. This led to Daryll working late nights, staying out after the club closed, and eventually not coming home at all. Things only got worse. We grew further and further apart. And then, one day about two o'clock in the morning, I opened the front door of the house and yelled out, "Help, someone call the police!" This was after Daryll had come home from a night of drinking and feasting over his cousin's house- knowing that my daughter and I had no food in the house and no transportation or money to go get anything. Needless to say, things got pretty heated when he finally decided to show up. Daryll, almost 300 pounds and six feet-four inches tall, yanked the phone out of my hand and then ripped it out of the wall to keep me from calling the police. He then commenced to pick me up by my collar with his hand around my neck and pushed me into several walls of the house. The police came and they left, taking Daryll with them. I filed for a restraining order against Daryll. I wish I could say that that was the end of that relationship, but it wasn't. I ended up taking him back on promises that he did not keep. We stayed together probably another four months before I packed up and left him for good. My daughter and I stayed with a church friend and her daughter for a while and later moved into our place. I didn't divorce right away since I was paying for it and money was scarce. Colorado was beautiful, but it was difficult to appreciate the beauty because of all the pain I was going through. Even though I never felt "in love" with Daryll, the separation felt like the ripping apart of souls and it was very painful. My daughter and I eventually moved back to the Midwest where we were able to reestablish ourselves and get the support we needed.

Since then, I have remarried and consider myself blessed to have someone who truly loves me and takes good care of me and my family. We've had some challenges in the beginning stages of our marriage, but love and determination kept us true to our vows. Twenty-seven years later, the kids are grown and my husband and I both are moving into new career endeavors. We have grown together and know the importance of communication and respect for each other. We understand boundaries. We understand "Me time." We understand that we both need to be "whole" to have a successful marriage.

~ Sophia

Sophia's journey gives light to the fact that we don't have to subscribe to the idea of life and love having a timeline. Her story narrates her full-circle moment reconnecting with, and marring her teenage crush. Her second chance at love took more than a decade to come together. Her husband of twenty-seven years was there in the beginning, before she had a child and before she found herself in an unhealthy marriage. Her happily ever after is dedicated to doing the hard work of building a marriage with the foundation of mutual respect for each other.

First, become whole within yourself.
Then, you can give love from a place of abundance.

VII

Genay's Story

I believe marriage is a beautiful institution. You have two parties who love one another and are willing to have each other's back and take care of one another. That's incredibly beautiful. To have someone who knows your shortcomings, yet is still willing to genuinely love you and help strengthen you to overcome your issues, is wonderful. I would consider that an important part of being blessed.

Today, my philosophy on marriage is that it's a long-lasting business; both parties need to enter into the binding contract wisely. My initial philosophy regarding marriage was that it consisted mostly of arguments and just an overall difficult time. I thought the only true purpose of it was to not be in a lifestyle of fornication. Before I was married, my views of marriage were shaped by my parents, who constantly fought; in combination with that, growing up, I can't recall seeing anyone "happily married". As I got older and began going to church, I noticed many of the women who were going to the altar for prayer were married women. They were the ones crying the hardest and seemingly needing the most help. Watching these women further solidified my belief that marriage was hard and difficult.

I got married to get it over with since I was somehow maintaining this relationship. I can't say I was happy to get married or "in love", I felt like I wasn't getting out of this relationship, so I thought, "let me go ahead with it". Naturally, how I felt was reflected in my actions, and thus didn't create the best recipe for a happy or loving marriage. My marriage consisted mostly of tolerance on my end rather than love. Yes, I loved my husband as a person, but I didn't want to be married to him, I just went along with things. I still tried to put forth the necessary effort, but it wasn't coming from the heart which made it seem like work (I didn't realize that at the time). When anything flows from the heart, it naturally produces what's needed at the right time, but when you have to conjure up feelings that don't exist, you're literally just going through the motions trying to do or say what you think should fit in a situation.

Within the first 6 months of my marriage, I was pregnant. Things weren't going well between us so we discussed separating after the baby was born. The plan was for me to get back working and save up some money after maternity leave. Things between us weren't going well because we argued often. In retrospect, it may have been due to my own frustrations of not really wanting to be there. I think that may have been the underlying cause of most of the issues we encountered. The arguments, of course, were birthed by small, dumb stuff like not cleaning up, not saying, "hello" when I came into the house, and not listening. Later on, after the baby was born, I recall paying attention to how often we argued and it was like literally every other day there was an argument. My plans for moving out became a bust because my car ended up breaking down and my license was all jacked up, so my husband was my ride to work and every place else.

Eventually, I got to the point where I began entertaining compliments from other men and things of that nature. I began talking to an old flame on and off again (about 3 years). I think talking to him helped me to deal with everything that was going on at home. Looking back, I feel like I used him to get through all of my issues I was facing at home. Naturally, I didn't want my husband to find out because I didn't want him to stop taking me to work, which would cause me to lose everything. After a while, he found out I was talking to another man; he called my mother and told her I needed a place to live because he was putting me out. I told him I wasn't going anywhere, but eventually I changed my mind and said I would leave. I figured he could deal with all the bills and everything else. Of course, he didn't like I agreed to leave. He then said he would leave, but he never did. I didn't completely stop talking to my old flame, just tried to be more careful. There were times when my husband and I tried to get on one accord and repair things, but there were too many hurtful comments that were always said (on both ends), which made it difficult to fully give it that valiant effort. Unfortunately, I didn't feel bad about talking to someone else. I didn't think I had hurt my husband in any way. I will admit that I did feel like a failure in having an extramarital affair. Keep in mind, at this point, we had only been talking on the phone and texting, so it was more of an emotional affair.

So right as I was on the cusp of getting my finances in order, and had lost my baby weight, I ended up sleeping with my husband (out of guilt from talking to another man) and getting pregnant AGAIN, which put me all the way back at square one along with a deep depression. My hair fell out and I was just in a bad place overall.

During this time I focused on taking care of my kids and going to work. Because we only had one car, I was always stuck at home or waiting for him. That situation made me realize how important it is to have a backup plan. I couldn't rely on my husband. He had his own issues and hurts that I inflicted on him. If the situation were reversed, I wouldn't have done anything for him if I knew he'd been talking to another woman. So in my opinion, he was a better person than me, because I would have handled things differently. I can't blame him for being mean to me during that time, but it definitely didn't help things. In my mind, I was just running a tab of why I didn't like him and why I wanted a divorce.

I got my license together and got a truck, and then I filed for divorce while we were living together, which he said he was blindsided by. He was very upset after being served. He said that although we discussed divorcing after our son's birth, he was never really serious about it; he thought we were just arguing. I told him we were both serious about the divorce, and perhaps he just forgot due to the many other fights and arguments that took place during the interim.

I don't feel like I was in the right to get a divorce because technically you should only divorce when there's infidelity or serious irreconcilable differences (drugs, beating, abandonment). I wasn't really praying during this time because I didn't want to hear the Holy Ghost tell me to stay. Plus, I wanted to get out there and hook up for real with my old flame that I had been chatting with for the past two years. In my mind, I deserved some fun and wanted to just be with my kids. My divorce was going fine, neither of us had anything worth fighting for so it was going smoothly until I missed the third court date and the judge dismissed the divorce. My husband mentioned during this time how nice I was towards him and how happy I was. I told him I never disliked him, I just didn't want to be married to him, and since there was no longer a need for the pretense, I could be myself.

I moved out and got an apartment. I started going to church again and just living my life peacefully. There was no fussing or arguing, and coming home to a clean kitchen was better than sex. I finally felt happy and free again. I went on a date with my old flame and realized I couldn't go back to the single life, so I ended it. I found a new church home. My kids and I were simply enjoying things. My husband and I were on decent terms since he lived close by, but eventually, he lost his job and then his place, soon he needed somewhere to live. I didn't want him to come with me, but at the same time I didn't want to see him on the streets. Again, I didn't dislike him, but I certainly didn't want to live with him because I didn't want to be subjected to or have to give an answer for my whereabouts. It was like getting out of prison for a few months, only to get locked back up again.

So he came back, and of course, he wanted to stay. He kept saying how he didn't want to lose his family. I'll admit things had fundamentally changed at this point because he needed to move into my place and because it was mine and not ours, my attitude was one of, '*if you don't like who I am or what I'm doing, feel free to leave*'. I made it clear by many demeaning comments that it wouldn't be a love lost of any kind. I was pretty mean and resented him living with me.

We had a few appointments to go to counseling, but we never made it. Even in the beginning when I suggested counseling, he wasn't interested because he felt that the counselor would somehow be biased.

I can't say at what point things got better, but I definitely began to look at myself more and more and repent of my own ways. When it came down to it, I needed to do better and be better. I couldn't change, fix, or make my spouse into what I wanted, but I did know what was required of me. I didn't want my lifestyle to be false. I didn't want to be fake and just an outright hypocrite. I've apologized to my husband of course for my actions, and the way I've handled things, and he has done the same. My husband admitted that his revenge on me was to make me fat. Since the majority of the cooking in our household was done by my husband, he said he would cook a lot of fatty foods and watch as I gained weight because he knew I would eat anything. He said he was going to leave a note when he died confessing what he did. As he watched me struggle with my weight, he felt guilty and admitted his plan. That has left me cautious and watchful about his cooking.

I've learned that love is a choice, and it's for the hard times, not just the good. I'm to love because God requires us to walk in love, not to be loved by someone. In order to be like God, we have to love and forgive. Marriage requires truth, maturity, humility, long-suffering (you will suffer), submission, and forgiveness. Over time, I've come to realize that no relationship is perfect, nor is any person. As we look at people and hear about their relationships, we sometimes covet what they have instead of learning to be content with what we have. I personally try to combat negative thoughts about my spouse by focusing on his positive attributes. My husband has said on many occasions if the Lord wants to dissolve this union he can do it without there being malice and animosity. I'm not sure what the future holds for us, but I'm doing my best to be honest and not just go along with things. And lastly, I'm choosing to love.

~Genay

Genay is married to a pastor. Her religious beliefs allowed her to maintain an open heart and mind. Genay shares her story to encourage readers to self-evaluate the part they play in their own happiness. Her story is one that speaks of overcoming the frustrations of marriage that could lead to divorce.

"Turn your wounds into wisdom."

-Oprah Winfrey

VIII

Sandra's Story

I am a nurse and I have six children; one before marriage and five during marriage. I grew up on the North Side of Chicago, in a small close knit community. I grew up mainly in a single parent household until my mother married my stepfather when I was fifteen years old.

I honestly got married for several reasons outside of my own will. Don't get me wrong, I loved the guy I was with, and I thought marriage should have been the next step. After all, I was pregnant with my second child and did not want to be a "statistic". At that time in my life, my partner and I were a part of the Muslim community. We were living together unmarried and pregnant, which was frowned upon. How the community viewed us carried a lot of weight in our lives, and they were instrumental in getting us married.

From the beginning, there were many red flags and abusive behaviors. I never had the guts to leave because I had already been kicked out of my home with no real plan of what to do next or where to go. My relationship was doomed from the start. I thought our new-found religion would help guide us, but unfortunately, that was not the case.

There were many lessons along the way, all very valuable and substantial in my growth as a mom, person, and human being. The journey has had the greatest impact on my self-growth. I have learned to trust myself, obey my intuitions, learn myself, and I have discovered peace. I learned to pray again, and put my worries, confusion, anger, hatred, and resentment into God's hands. I learned strength and how to rely on myself and almighty God. I also learned that some things are not worth fighting for, because in the end you lose more than you actually gain.

I wish I would have left the relationship before marriage, but I also understand the marriage journey brought me to be the person I am today; otherwise, I'm not sure if I would have been equipped to handle the breakdown of my relationship.

About 8-12 months prior to our separation, I started to notice my ex was getting excited about some female attention he was receiving at work. I would hear the same name periodically. He also started to communicate with females he reconnected with online. His attitude changed, and he became careless. However, he started to accuse me of cheating, and he questioned my behavior. He was dissatisfied with his life, his family, his career, and his lack of the things he wanted. We did not exhaust all possibilities before deciding to separate. Although I mourned the loss of my relationship, my marriage, and my family, it was a dead relationship and never should have lasted as long as it had. After being separated for 6-7 months, I tried to get my ex to consider counseling. He said, no, and at that point, I looked, and moved forward. Within the next year, I filed for both divorce and child support, and that is when the fighting began. The children were with me and we did not have any type of visitation schedule set-up. When he had to pay child support, the shit hit the fan and all gloves were off!

One day, in the midst of our battle, he decided to invite me to dinner. He spoke about a life we could have together and the money we could make. We discussed a new house and all this stuff. However, he never said he was sorry, nor did he mention that he loved me or missed me. It was a sad day. I sat in the restaurant that day and cried. It felt like it was a trick, but I also felt bad that I didn't want to go back to that relationship or that life; it was hard but I said, "no."

After my divorce, I started to go out more and travel when I could. I partied and drank alcohol more than I ever had in my life. Prior to that, my life consisted of work, being a wife, taking care of children, and all things children related like homework, school, recitals, games, and conferences.

During this period of my life, I didn't really experience depression. I was terribly angry, upset, hurt, disappointed, embarrassed, but not depressed (clinically). I was very sad for a time, but eventually overcame it. If I am to think about my mental state now, I feel mentally stable. I do overthink people's reaction towards me. I have a tendency to over analyze conversations and different interactions with people, but the great thing is, I am still interested in getting married again. It will be a different marriage next time. I don't have small children anymore, so I would not be cooking and cleaning every day. It would be a marriage that honors both people. Respect, kindness, love, and compassion would establish our base.

While going through my divorce, I received plenty of advice. I wouldn't say I received terrible advice, but I would say a lot of advice came prematurely, which made it hard for me to process it at the stage of loss or grief I was in at that time. Timing is very important, so don't underestimate it! The best advice I did take was to look out for myself; to stop caring about what others needed, because when I look out for me, that takes care of others.

My ex and I can, and hopefully will, become friends later in life. It just takes time to arrive at the same place at the same time. At this point we are not friends. Many times I have gotten burned, hurt, manipulated, and/or taken advantage of by my ex. It seems a friendship between us will be a little tough, but not impossible.

The advice I would give to someone who is going through something similar, is to first take care of yourself on all levels; mentally, spiritually, physically, emotionally, sexually, socially, and financially. My next piece of advice would be to take one to two years off from dating. Lastly, be safe.

~ Sandra

Sandra's ability to appreciate the person she is today, as her story includes heartache and some desire to do things differently, reminds us that everything serves a purpose. We can choose to grow from our experiences and use that to validate our journey to loving ourselves.

"Every problem is a gift-without problems
we would not grow."

-Tony Robbins

IX

Farrah's Story

I met my ex when I was sixteen and he was nineteen, we dated for nearly a year before he left for college. When he was away, we moved on separately. Years later, I was showing a colleague one of my old photo books and as she was scanning the photos, she saw a picture of a man, my ex, and said that he looked familiar. She said his name, and I confirmed that it was him. She then told me that he worked at AT&T, which was nearby. A week later she called him while we were at work and transferred him to my line. Him and I had a great conversation that day so we made plans to hang out. When we met, he was so much fun. At the time, I had a three-year-old daughter and he had a son. Although I was in my early twenties, I felt like I was ready for this relationship.

In the beginning, my ex was such a gentleman. He knew how to make me laugh, he was a great dresser, and he was charismatic. I started to invite him to family gatherings as things got serious. Family is extremely important to me, and he got along easily with my very large family. After five or six months, he proposed at a restaurant. I felt it was too fast, I wasn't in love with him, but I liked him a lot, so I said, "yes". Early in our relationship, I noticed red flags. The first red flag was when he told me I couldn't get my nails done because we needed to save money. I suggested that he stopped getting haircuts if I was going to have to stop getting my nails done. We argued over that topic, and I told him he could leave. He was shocked at my response and calmed down. After we got married, he told me to quit my job, this was another red flag. I understood why he suggested it, but it made no sense financially. He wanted me to quit because I used to date one of my coworkers.

The dismantlement of our relationship happened when he failed to keep a job. He had over 20 jobs while we were together, but was never able to keep them for some strange reason. He was a healthy young man, so I was genuinely concerned about his work ethic. Later, I found out there were times he'd leave the house claiming he was on his way to work, but he would never actually go. I was extremely frustrated and instead of telling him how he really made me feel, I stepped out of our marriage. I admit I was wrong for that. The guy I was drawn to was everything my ex wasn't, and during that time, he appealed to me. Unbeknownst to me, my ex was also having an affair. Eventually, I found out and we discussed working on our marriage since we were both guilty. This is when the suffering started.

Although I was the breadwinner, he continued to meet with other women. The little money he made when he chose to work, went to other women. We had one vehicle and he held it hostage. I was often left alone with the kids while he hung out. One day, he was at a restaurant with another woman and someone my sister knew had recorded him. The video showed him sitting at the bar with his hand on the woman's lower back. My sister showed me the video for confirmation that it was indeed him; it was. That evening I waited for him to return home. When he came home, I asked him about his outing and he denied doing anything. I lost my cool momentarily and lunged at him. I tried to bite him. I was hurt and felt that the open disrespect was cruel. I knew that he had to go. I could not take it anymore. I think of our downfall and believe that although it was dramatic, I would separate in the same manner even though it was ugly and nasty. I felt that I needed that moment. I'll never take him back.

We had three different therapists, both together and separately during our marriage. We exhausted all efforts to mend our relationship. The last counselor was a pastor that my ex chose. I'm sure he chose the pastor because he assumed the pastor would be bias and support him. Either way, in the end, we could not be helped.

I found relief during our separation. My financial burdens were lifted. I moved in with my mother and I was able to save money. I felt healthy and stress-free. My kids didn't have to live in a home filled with tense anxiety.

I feel like I received lots of advice from people. My aunt told me that my ex is not my friend, and after a while, I realized what she meant. I chose to listen to positive people on YouTube and I read self-help books. At times, I felt that many people wanted to hear the drama, but they did not always have my best interest at the forefront of their advice. I've experienced some toxic behavior, but I would definitely get married again. I wish we could have truly worked out our issues because I believe in the institution of marriage.

~ Farrah

Farrah found peace in being able to remove herself from the unhealthy environment that her marriage became. Her story reminds us that it is okay to own our emotions no matter how ugly they are. The important part is to remove yourself and regroup, which is how she found contentment.

"The pain will subside, and the moment will become a learning experience that just adds vibrancy to your story."

-Liza

X

Liza's Story

I have always been a person of great passion and energy. I love hard and in some ways, I tend to reciprocate whatever mood I get from a person; I am aware this isn't always a good thing. This reciprocity is what possibly led to the shift in my life a few years ago. I have two children with my ex-husband. We've known one another since I was fourteen years old. We started a serious relationship our senior year in high school and went to college together. Prior to our divorce, we were together, inclusive of dating and marriage, for fifteen years.

While married, I believed that I curated a beautiful life for my small family. My story is one where I loved him deeply and thought I'd die without him; spoiler alert- I didn't die. I was codependent and the silent partner in everything great that he had ever done. Although I never wanted to be a single mother, here I am. Crazy thing is I'm still me, except I'm no longer codependent nor am I the silent partner.

In the book, *The Seven Secrets To Healthy, Happy Relationships* by Don Miguel Jr and Heatherash Mara, they stated that perceptions of events dictate your current situation. Although this may be common knowledge, it is worth rementioning on account that it is a reminder that your mind holds the power to where you are currently in life. I had to change how I viewed my divorce in order for me to heal. I realized I was able to love him as long as I needed to. I didn't have to stop loving him because he had moved on. I did, however, have to understand that he wasn't going to come back to me. So, I had to figure out how I planned to handle that reality. I needed to figure out how I was going to perceive my new life; was it going to be a tale of tragedy or redemption?

I believe that my general idea of love first came from my grandmother. She seemed to genuinely care about my well-being. My grandmother had nearly a hundred grandchildren and great-grandchildren from her own fourteen children, yet, I was often held and rocked by her. When she held me, she let me rub her soft, nearly translucent skin while I sucked my thumb, and she often gave me so many kisses that I felt like she loved me best. As rambunctious as I was, she had never yelled at me. She thought everything I did was sweet and she loved my energy. My God, that woman was perfection. As an adult, I realize that patience, acceptance, and open communication is how I show love, and ironically it was the love I remember my grandmother showing me.

When it came to marriage, I thought love was about procreating and staying in a relationship no matter what. It seemed like that was my parent's method. It had nothing to do with partnership nor goals. My parents had six children and although our household did run efficiently, there was not a lot of open communication. Eventually, they divorced when I was fourteen and the youngest was four years old. Needless to say, the youngest had a completely different life than us older children.

In my own relationship, love was an action verb. It was being with family, hitting milestones, and going on dates. While that is part of love, it is still a small percentage. My ex and I had never learned to fight fair or gracefully. We grew up together and practically shared the same upbringing, and seemingly the same morals and values, but those morals and values were incomplete and riddled with hypocrisy. They were false maps laid out for us by broken people, and still we followed them. There were times we attempted to shift our beliefs by reading self-help books, but by then, we were too far gone.

So when people ask, *why did you get married?* The short answer for me would be, because I was asked. Please note, I was completely in love and we were together several years prior to marriage. Initially, he and I weren't in a rush to marry. We had both agreed that marriage led to divorce, and because of that, we were uninterested in rushing down the aisle. So when he asked, I was not only surprised, but a bit nervous and filled with anxiety. As a couple, we'd spoke about marrying one day, and I even knew the type of ring I wanted, but I was still shocked when he proposed. The idea of being "good enough to marry" did eventually bring me joy. I remember saying to him that marriage meant we'd be together forever, and fight through everything as a unit. He confirmed his understanding, so a beautiful wedding was planned.

Things fell apart immediately after we came to realize that lies were being told between us, and it was not long after we married. Something we had never experienced before. I noticed a consistent behavior change in my ex-husband about a year prior to our separation. He missed every extended family outing in 2016; he claimed he was working. This caused the dismantlement of everything we had co-created. For a while, I silently knew of his indiscretions as he lied to me often. I didn't want my life nor lifestyle to change, but eventually I confided in a male colleague and he gave me male-perspective. I cried to him often and he was a great pillar during that time. As luck would have it, I fell for him. At that time, I felt my actions were validated. My ex had cheated many times, with more than one woman. I had never betrayed our relationship until I knew he had done so first; someone confirmed his imprudent behavior to me via Facebook chat.

During that time, I was constantly reactive, and I continued to reciprocate what I received. It was so unhealthy, but it was part of who I was at that time. If my ex decided to not come home for four hours, then when he finally came home, I'd leave for the same amount of time. We began to be disrespectful and careless. After that, the rage between us was too intense to live under the same roof. When you're both equally ill-tempered, it is best to separate until help is sought. The downfall of our union was hard, and it went on nonstop until we were divorced. The biggest lesson I learned was to not lose myself completely in the midst of chaos. I was always fighting so hard for everything, for attention, for peace, for love, and for my relationship overall. It got unhealthy for our entire family. I'd never do that again. I've learned such independence, and realized that I was just as educated, intelligent, and capable as he. As cliché as it is, I had lost him and found myself.

One thing that perplexed me for a long time was not exhausting all possibilities to repair our marriage. In the end, when help was needed, he didn't want to do anything but separate. That hurt me because it further proved that we did not love on the same level. It made no sense to me, because we'd never experienced pain like we had, but we separated within a month of us experiencing everything. He had moved on fairly quickly, and I decided to do the same. I decided to close myself off from the world to deal with the internal pain I felt. I shut down social media and declined invites. For a while, I only had enough energy to go to work and then back home. There was no point in fighting for a person who wasn't fighting for me.

I didn't go through a reckless phase, but I made a reckless decision. I did settle down with someone immediately after my divorce was finalized, and it lasted a few years. I can openly say that I loved that person with a freshness that was exhilarating. I learned another life lesson that allowed me to re-evaluate how I viewed love and healthy relationships.

Going through my divorce was the hardest thing I've ever experienced. I was grieving for an extended period of time and then I was suddenly tired of myself. I replayed my old life and glamorized the time I spent with my ex. I had to encourage myself by limiting the amount of time I spent ruminating over the past. I decided to go out one Friday night, and that night changed my life. My friend and I decided to go out every other Friday night from then on, and that is where I acquired a new group of friends. While married, we hung out with other married people. Occasionally, I was still hanging out with those friends, but I kept getting emotional because I was always alone in those group settings. People were walking on eggshells because some of them were friends with my ex too; it was uncomfortable and at times, disheartening. Meeting new people allowed for growth, both mentally and emotionally.

I have a strong mental state as of now, but that doesn't mean that I don't backslide or that I am smiling all the time. I think once you've gone through a major heartbreak or grief, you're better equipped to survive in this world. I will not play victim in this life. I don't want an excuse placed upon me that further inhibits my ability to take responsibility for my life. I find myself recalibrating at times. This self-awareness has made me tap into old hobbies and realize that I should seek things outside of my head when I feel an upheaval of emotion. I have found a way to recognize triggers and I decide to avoid them.

Worst advice I've ever received was, "take everything from him". That advice was low-class and senseless. I would rather children see a loving father than further uproot their life by waging war in a courtroom. I also find it mentally beneficial to have a break from my children. Shared custody is a blessing in many ways. I grew closer to my daughter, because with me being the only parent in the house while she was with me, she was forced to be less of a daddy's girl and more of a momma's baby (my son has always been a momma's boy).

The best advice I had received was that I should not expect karma to make his life more difficult because I was hurting.

I was told that I may never see him hurt or struggle, and I'd have to come to peace with that and stop being bitter. A man told me that matter-of-factly, and I stopped at that very moment. I was done being bitter and I chose to overcome my daily sadness. I can now say, I would be friends with my ex down the road because we have found a calm, at the moment it isn't consistent, but it is possible because I have developed a different form of love for him.

I was given grace several times during my separation until post-divorce. The more I came out of my shock and anger, the more mature I grew. The more observant I became. The more responsible I wanted to be. I just became more. I grew independent of assistance, and enjoyed running my own life. I knew where I was headed and I understood what needed adjustment in my life and attitude. Shifting my outlook made me grateful for my downfall. I now have experience and a story to tell which is why I would get married again. I'm not anxious to find a husband, but I do think companionship comes easy to me, and I would enjoy a man designed for my life.

I savor the lessons I've learned and I'd like to remind anyone going through a break-up that the rumors are true, only time heals- so the trick is to fill that space with people and things that help you grow. Don't focus on seeking revenge. Remove yourself from social outlets that hinder your development. In the midst of heartache allow yourself to mourn because the pain will subside, and the moment will become a learning experience that just adds vibrancy to your story.

~Liza

Liza's story depicts the different facets of love and the levels of pain that can follow. Her ability to realize that her sadness would not be remedied through the misery of her ex allowed her to be free from the consuming nature of bitterness. She holds her growth and maturity very highly and that has become her pursuit to her happiness.

"Love yourself unconditionally, just as you love those closest to you despite their flaws."

-Les Brown

XI

⚜

Nicole's Story

The impact of societal norms barely makes sense as an adult. As a child and then as a teenager and even as a young adult, I only saw that everyone I knew had strived to make a family, and then hold on to a family, no matter how unhealthy or toxic it was. That, I believe, is why I got married.

I cannot say why things fell apart or that they fell apart at all...they were never together. We did what we saw many before us do, and we tried to maintain. The kids, the house, the cars, the careers, and the silent baggage that was never unpacked.

The greatest lesson learned from my divorce is both simple and complicated simultaneously. It is easy enough to understand that someone else's insecurities should not decide your every action, but how very complex it is to extricate yourself from a cycle that has been witnessed as the norm.

During what I think of as my transition, my most

significant area of growth has been relearning what it means to be me. Finding the resolve to make my own needs meaningful, to not bend my desires because of the demands of everyone around me.

Looking back, the only thing I would have done differently in the dismantling of my marriage is to make it happen sooner. The answer is probably cliché, but ripping the Band-Aid off would have saved heartache, pain, time, and money.

As with why things fell apart, the changes in us that brought light to our challenges were no changes at all; they were there from the start. For my ex-husband to feel assured as a provider, I had to take a pay cut and scale back in my career. To feel secure in his lack of self-confidence, I had to be a lesser version of myself. I had to give more of myself than was available, leaving nothing for my family and less than nothing for myself.

There were no possibilities to exhaust in saving my marriage, but I tried anyway. Counseling, vacations, self-help books, giving, taking, changing, evolving, stretching, and finally, nothing. Desperation for us turned into determination for me.

When the separation was final, I didn't go through the phases I have seen many people go through during a divorce. The traumatic ending of the relationship, coupled with a double mastectomy that almost took my life, gave me more than enough *right now* stress. I could not find the capacity to find a habit.

Depression was definitely part of my journey. As a woman, I found a lot of blame to place on myself. I took every opportunity to see what I could or should have done to achieve a different outcome. I just knew that there could have been a more orchestrated exit that was less complicated and less emotional. Believe it or not, I wanted efficiency. I coped with the depression by doing what I had always been taught, regardless of the circumstance, to keep going. I don't say this as a good thing; my fifteen year-old daughter recently pointed out to me that not everyone is built to push everything down and keep going. I now recognize this as not a coping skill but as automation in despondency.

My current philosophy on marriage is not a philosophy at all. I simply appreciate seeing the love that gives its receivers growth, enhances joy, and supports in providing peace. I don't see love as an emotion, but rather a choice. A decision that may or may not be mutual.

The worst advice I was ever given was to be submissive, take what was given until the Lord changed my husband's heart. The twenty years that endured for the speaker's husband to become a good husband and father didn't seem so long to her at the time. It seemed like a death sentence to me.

The best advice I was ever given was to be kind to myself and understand that I can feel what I am feeling without judgment. I must remind myself daily that I deserve kindness and I deserve love.

Being married does not appeal to me as much as simply loving someone and being loved equally in return. Marriage is complicated, and the idea of marriage is even more so. The concept of marriage ingrained in us as children, and what marriage is now, is too at odds to reconcile for me.

My ex-spouse and I have no place in each other's lives anymore, if we ever did. Being friends is beyond a possibility for us; the damage that has been done was irreparable. Divorce is usually messy, but sometimes the echoing pain reaches levels that will always be heard.

My advice to anyone going through a transition would be that you deserve kindness, especially from yourself. Many obstacles will beat up on you before your journey is made; sometimes, you will be the only kindness you receive, lavish it upon yourself.

~Nicole White

In Nicole's story we hear her point out the suggestion that your idea of love and examples of relationships that are normalized in our youth play a role in how we function in our marriages. Her most important relationship, in the end, was the one she developed with herself. Through self-compassion and kindness, her journey is one that allows for a greater sense of self awareness.

Give yourself grace, be kind to yourself
through the process of finding your new normal.

XII

⸿

Rodney's Story

I didn't know what love was. I wasn't given any examples. I knew what love wasn't, from what I saw growing up. As a single mother, mom did the best she could, but I knew that I didn't want my children to grow up the way I did. I knew when I had kids I didn't want them in poverty. I wanted them to have the two-parent household I didn't have.

I got married because I was in love. She was the one. I wanted to make an honest man out of myself, and I didn't want to play house for years. To me, it didn't make sense to build with someone and not get married. I had my days of messing around and I was tired of that, so it was important to settle down and start building with someone.

We just celebrated seven years of marriage, and we had been together since we were teenagers. After getting comfortable with the things we were able to accomplish, as a couple, our vision eventually got lost. We started to pay attention to what everyone else was doing and what was going on outside of our marriage. We didn't have a common goal and it's easy to get caught up in what everyone is doing on social media. We were content, and things became routine. We all know how easy someone can come in and tell you the things you want to hear, especially when you're feeling like something is missing. The forbidden becomes more attractive when you've become complacent at home.

When you've been with someone for as long as we were, you notice everything. Our conversations began to change, and her habits shifted. Her attitude, the music she listened to, and even the words she would say. I noticed a shift in it all. Sure, I've been tempted, but I never was willing to put everything at risk.

My first thought was, you gotta be stupid! We had so much going on. How could she step out on me? I didn't feel my real feelings until a couple of months later. I was more angry than anything at first until reality sank in around that September. That was the first time I cried. What do I need to do? How do I pick up the pieces? How can I work this out to be able to see my kids? That was the most important thing.

I gave her an ultimatum. Quit your job or we're done. I got the paperwork to file for the divorce, but we continued to try to work on our marriage. She didn't quit and continued to talk to the guy. At that point, I decided to do my thing as well. She eventually moved out of our home, because the tension was high, and the respect was gone. That was a significant point between us.

My pride was touched. I felt like I didn't deserve what she did. I was devoted to my family, and couldn't understand why this happened to me. Moving out meant that we were "officially-unofficationally" done, the house was mine and I could do what I wanted to do-so I dated.

I did want to give things a fair shot. There was a lot of back and forth before I decided to actually file for divorce. We went to counseling, and I felt like I kept trying to make things work. She had even moved back home, but it just wasn't coming together. I actually filed for a divorce a year and a half after we separated. When I filed, I was relieved. I got tired of trying and feeling so unhappy. I was done and my mind was made up. The best advice I got was to "do something different." The back and forth wasn't working, so I began to move differently. I started to set boundaries.

She was back at the house; it was easier for the kids. She slept downstairs and we were separate under the same roof. I was getting ready to leave one day and she looked at me, put her head in her hand, started to cry, and said, "I can't." It wasn't that she cried. It was the way she looked at me. She looked at me like it was the summer of 2004 when she rolled up on me on Andrews Avenue and shot me down to get my number. Me being who I am, I felt like my effort to be a good man should be recognized. At that moment, I felt like she got it. I felt like it hit, and I was willing to see if she was for real.

If I could've done things differently, I wish I would've kept my cool. I do believe that no matter how messy things get, everything serves a purpose. There was so much at stake and emotions were high. It was hard to try to make sense of how to move forward when I felt like I was the only one trying to piece it together. I made a lot of emotional decisions.

My biggest takeaway was to never let anyone take you for

granted. I am the shit! I know who I am, and what I bring to the table. I would never let anyone make me feel less than that, again. On one hand, I appreciate my family so much more but I'm also aware that the unexpected can happen at any time.

I stayed in the gym and leaned on my circle during that time, heavily. I was focused on improving myself. As the OGs would tell me, marriage is hard work. I think you have to be intentional about being a better person before getting married to make a marriage stand the test of time. You have to be willing to have open communication. You gotta talk.

~Rodney

Rodney showed us the redemptive power of love. Your willingness to look beyond your own pride and expose your vulnerability can lead you to a path where you find a new depth and greater possibilities. He was willing to maintain what he worked hard to build through forgiveness and understanding. Rodney's happily ever after isn't without flaws but remains his truth. He remains committed to making his marriage work.

We get to choose whether we grow from our experiences or go through them in vain.

XIII

The End

Life continues to move forward. The end of a marriage, as you knew it, can be the beginning of a beautiful journey of self-discovery, validation, and self-awareness. We can't always anticipate what difficulties may come our way, but through reflection, we can approach life with a better perspective.

While everyone's stories were uniquely their own, there were certainly some common themes that were clear throughout. As the saying goes, *hindsight is 20/20*. As each writer was given the opportunity to reflect on their life, it was evident that there are some common truths that helped each person get through what was a very difficult time for them.

Self-care is a must and a necessary part of healing. A large part of being married means that you are sacrificing certain pieces of your own desires in order to consider your spouse and children. Going through a separation or divorce requires you to devote a lot of energy toward surviving emotionally. So after you've sacrificed during your marriage and then found yourself in survival mode, self-care isn't naturally a priority.

It takes a concerted effort to invest in yourself and do it consistently. For our writers, it meant doing things that ultimately helped them become more self-aware and independent. They traveled, read, and surrounded themselves with people who supported them.

One of the less normalized acts of self-care, that our writers discovered, was forgiveness. They did not become consumed by the behavior of their exes or spouse but forgave them and forgave themselves. By doing that, they released the weight of their past and have been able to discover a better version of themselves.

Introspection is the starting point for moving forward. Doing a self-evaluation as you approach the road to a new normal is about understanding you. There is nothing like the breakdown of a marriage to prompt you to evaluate the direction of your life. The writers had to do internal evaluations on how they processed through their most critical moments.

What is being whole? More than once this idea was shared by the writers. They were able to recognize a lack of fully gaining a grasp on oneself before attempting to make a life commitment to someone else. Wholeness is unity within yourself. It is experiencing life through seeing ourselves with acceptance: flaws and all.

What did you gain from reading these experiences? What will be your bold attempt to fearlessly find your footing while establishing your new normal? What is your reset? What will you need to come to terms with so that you can be free and at peace? What have you learned? How does your circle support you? What can you bring with you into a new way of doing life and what do you need to leave behind? Your answers to these questions, and others, assist in shaping your journey forward to your *Happily Ever After.*

XIV

About the Authors

Xavia Jones

Xavia is the Co-Founder and Co-CEO at Fifth Street. As a storyteller, author, and business strategist, her passion for writing and business collide. In addition, she is the Creative Director for Fifth Street. She and her four children reside in the northwest suburbs of Chicago, Illinois.

Nicole White

As the Co-Founder and Co-CEO at Fifth Street, Nicole is also a mother, a nurse, and a lover of language. She is a higher education instructor with a Master's-level Nursing degree and psychology background. Nicole is passionate about helping others tell their story.

Lynda Wheeler

Lynda serves on the Board of Directors of Fifth Street Publishing and is the acquisitions, and editing manager. She holds a Bachelor's of Arts in English. Lynda is most creative when inspired by true events. A lover of wit and humor, she finds joy in creative writing, learning fun facts, and socializing.